Government
and You

by Lisa Harkrader

A government runs a town, state, or country. People make up the government.

▼ People vote for government leaders.

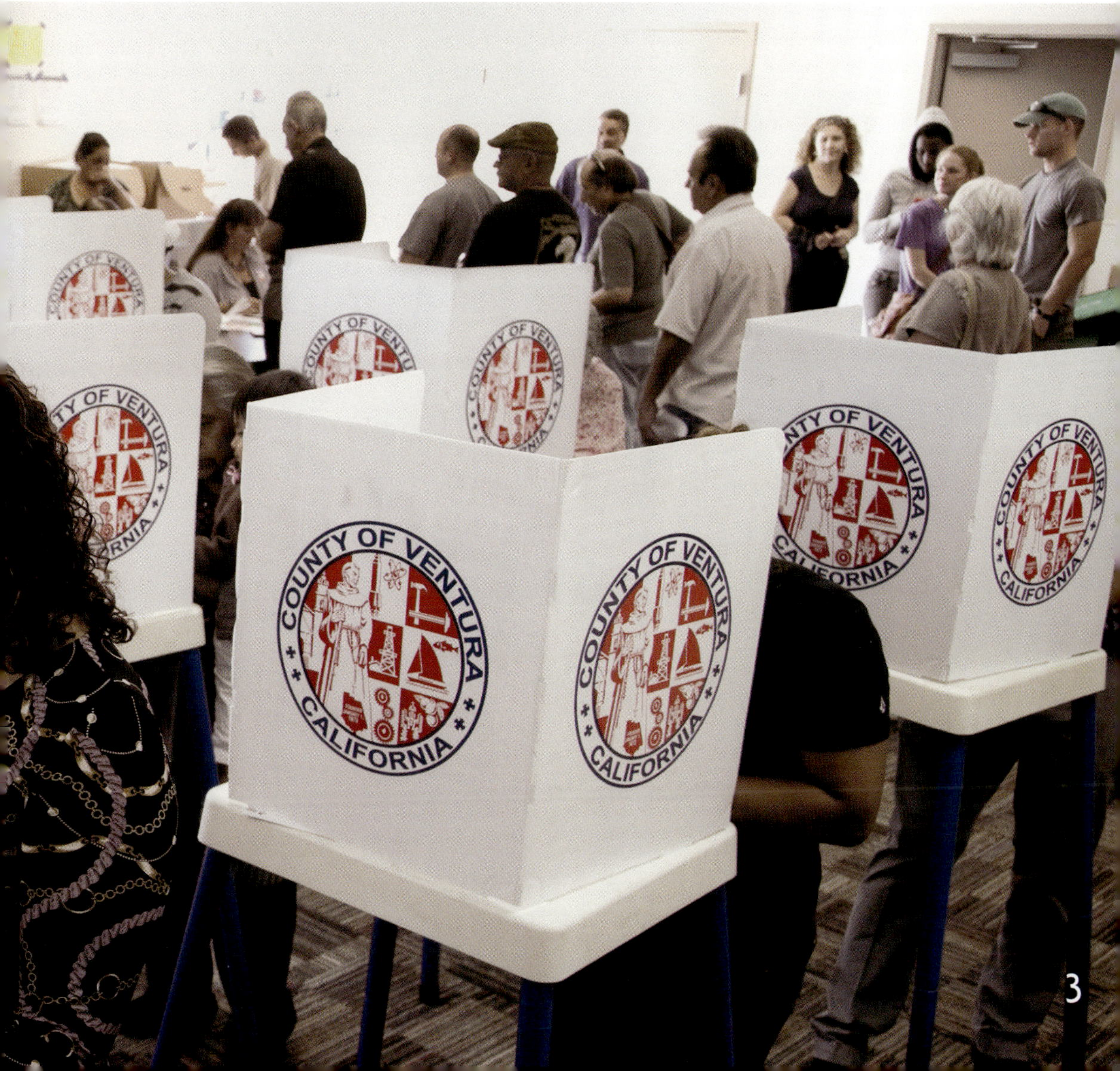
COUNTY OF VENTURA
CALIFORNIA

People in the government make and pass laws. Laws are rules we must follow.

▼ These people make the rules for a city or town.

5

One law tells people to drive slowly near a school.

▲ Some laws keep children safe at school.

Another law makes sure people in wheelchairs can enter buildings easily.

▲ This is a law that requires buildings to have handicap ramps.

Some laws also say what rights or freedoms we have.

We have the right to say what we want. We have the right to be treated fairly. We have many other rights.

▲ Courts are part of our government. A court decides if someone has broken the law.

Some laws make sure our food is safe to eat. Some laws keep our air and water clean.

▲ Our government tests water to make sure it is safe.

▲ Firefighters put out fires in burning buildings.

Some government workers keep us safe, too. Police officers and firefighters are government workers.

11

A government helps people have things they need.

▲ Some government workers take care of parks to keep them clean and safe.

▲ Each day, the post office sends millions of letters.

For example, people need schools and libraries. They need roads and bridges. They need post offices to send their mail.

13

People need garbage trucks to take away their trash. They need power lines and people to fix them.

Governments often do things that are difficult for people to do alone.

▲ Families can't fix their own power lines.

A government can help a town, state, and country run better.

▲ School crossing guards are government workers.